Robert Francis Kennedy had a marvelous sense of humor. Whether on the campaign trail or at a press conference; speaking to students or to businessmen, he delighted in seeing his audience laugh.

He was able, through his warm and gently teasing humor, to draw a shy child out of its shell or relax a tension-ridden meeting. His wit blossomed even at formal occasions and was in particular evidence at those memorable times when he was relaxing with family and friends.

As his brother Jack's campaign manager, as Attorney General, as Senator from New York, and finally as an aspiring Presidential candidate, Robert Francis Kennedy eased his life and the lives of those around him with his delightful sense of humor.

From this collection of Robert Kennedy's wit you will gain a deeper insight into this remarkable man and the life he led.

BILL ADLER
New York City

THE ROBERT F. KENNEDY WIT

Edited by
BILL ADLER

A BERKLEY MEDALLION BOOK
published by
BERKLEY PUBLISHING CORPORATION

OTHER BOOKS BY BILL ADLER

THE KENNEDY WIT
*
THE STEVENSON WIT
*
THE CHURCHILL WIT

I am most grateful to the editorial staff of Bill Adler Books, Inc., for their assistance in the preparation of this book. I am especially grateful to Catherine J. Greene and Martha Crisalli.

PHOTOGRAPHS COURTESY
UNITED PRESS INTERNATIONAL

BERKLEY MEDALLION EDITION, DECEMBER, 1968
BERKLEY MEDALLION BOOKS *are published by*
Berkley Publishing Corporation
200 Madison Avenue, New York, N.Y. 10016
BERKLEY MEDALLION BOOKS ® TM 757, 375
Printed in the United States of America

Table of Contents

On the Campaign Trail

During his campaign for the Democratic Presidential nomination, Senator Kennedy kept his audiences entertained with his frequent flashes of humor. While campaigning in Nebraska he informed his listeners, "President Johnson once said to me, 'Go west, young man.' I thought he was trying to tell me something, because I was in California at the time."

Campaigning for the Democratic Presidential nomination, Senator Kennedy spoke before several hundred prominent businessmen of Portland, Oregon. Realizing he was not in friendly territory, he told them:

"One of the business journals took a poll among 500 businessmen on who they favored for President. I got one vote and I understand they are looking for him."

When speaking to students at Kansas State University in March, 1968, Senator Kennedy explained his reasons for entering the Presidential race. He also told the audience that he had offered to stay out of the race if President Johnson named a commission with the power to change policies concerning the Vietnam war. The President rejected his offer, and Kennedy continued:

"Really, the only difference between us is that *I* wanted Senator Mansfield, Senator Fulbright, and Senator Morse appointed to the commission. And President Johnson, in his own inimitable style, wanted to appoint General Westmoreland, John Wayne, and Martha Raye."

Campaigning for the Democratic Presidential nomination Senator Kennedy spent some time in Huron, South Dakota, the birthplace of one of his opponents, Hubert Humphrey. Alluding to the profession of Humphrey's father, Kennedy joked:

"I want Hubert Humphrey to have any political position he wants except President. And if *I* am elected President with the help of the people of South Dakota, I will fill all my prescriptions at Humphrey's drugstore."

When campaigning, Senator Kennedy often enjoyed telling the crowds of a brief conversation he had with a Mother Superior at a previous stop:

"She said she had been praying to St. Jude for me. I thanked her—then asked somebody who St. Jude was. I learned that he is the patron saint of impossible causes."

At the 1968 New York Film Critics annual dinner, Kennedy announced that there was interest in remaking the film *The Good, The Bad and The Ugly,* "starring President Johnson, Gene McCarthy and myself—but the casting hasn't been determined yet."

In May, 1968, a reporter asked Kennedy if he would be willing to run as Vice-President with President Johnson. Kennedy later recounted:

"I explained to him that I thought a coalition government is possible in Saigon—But not here."

Campaigning in the birthplace of his Republican opponent in the 1964 Senatorial race, Robert Kennedy used the ironic situation to chide Senator Keating: "It gives me a deep sense of satisfaction to come here to Rochester, since I know it is the home town of a distinguished white-haired American . . . and I am referring, of course, to Susan B. Anthony."

Followed everywhere in his 1964 Senatorial campaign by charges of carpetbagging, Robert Kennedy would reply in terms like these: "I was raised in New York and went to school here. If somebody's going to vote against me because of my accent, there's really nothing I can do about it. It's really a Glen Cove accent, you know."

A substantial crowd turned out to greet Kennedy on his campaign stop at Syracuse, New York, in 1964. As the candidate moved down the line shaking hands, he was perplexed to find that the number of welcomers seemed to increase, not decrease. At last he hit upon the explanation: "As soon as they shake my hand, they run to the end of the line."

During the summer of 1964 a number of celebrities sponsored an outdoor campaign rally in support of Robert F. Kennedy for senator. At one point in the exuberant goings-on Kennedy joined his friend Sammy Davis, Jr. for a lovely duet and cracked, "If things don't go well on November third, we can go on tour."

Soon after Senator Kennedy declared his candidacy for the 1968 Democratic Presidential nomination, he spoke before a group of businessmen. Commenting on his candidacy, he remarked:

"I'm among friends here, and I'm among friends in the Senate, and they are wondering why I want to leave."

During his 1968 campaign for the Democratic Presidential nomination, Senator Robert Kennedy spoke before a large group of students at Berkeley, California. He predicted that Berkeley would have the greatest football team because "they've found a way of putting cleats on sandals."

During April, 1968, Senator Kennedy addressed a group of students at the University of San Francisco. A student asked him what he would do as President to solve the nation's problems. Kennedy replied:

"The only person who can really find the answers is probably God—and He's not running."

"I know not everybody thinks I'm a very strong candidate. But there are some who think I can win. George Hamilton called last night and asked me for my daughter's telephone number."

From a campaign speech
Alabama
June 16, 1968

On January 12, 1967, Senator Robert Kennedy addressed the Democratic Delegates to New York State's Constitutional Convention in Albany. After referring to the nearly miraculous work of the Constitutional Convention at Philadelphia in 1787, Kennedy went on to ask:

"Can we have a miracle at Albany? Perhaps our commitment to separation of church and state prevents that kind of goal—but I will tell you—for the kind of money New York is spending, we have a right to ask each of the delegates to seek *some* providential guidance...."

Senator Kennedy enjoyed recounting anecdotes about his campaign trails and particularly one concerning his 1964 Senatorial campaign. As he tells it, he was speaking before a large crowd in upstate New York, when he spotted a sign being enthusiastically waved aloft by a politically precocious young man about eight ears of age. The sign read, "Don't use *me* in your cynical power grab."

During the 1964 Senatorial campaign Robert Kennedy got the most enthusiastic reception in Rochester, New York. Thousands of screaming and cheering supporters lined the streets. Standing on top of his car, Kennedy placidly observed, "There's nothing like a quiet evening in Rochester."

Aware that he was a controversial candidate who either inspired deep loyalty or deep hate, Robert Kennedy observed during the 1968 cam-

paign for the Democratic Presidential nomination, "I am the only candidate opposed by both big business *and* big labor!"

As soon as his 1964 Senate victory had been assured, Robert Kennedy fulfilled his campaign promise to return to his very first stop on the campaign trail. At 3:30 a.m. on the morning following his election, he traveled down to the famed Fulton Fish Market on Manhattan's Lower East Side. Remarked a relieved Kennedy, "It smells a lot better down here now."

During Robert Kennedy's 1964 Senatorial campaign (which ran concurrently with the Presidential campaign) he received a particularly warm response to a speech given in Jamestown, New York. He acknowledged it with the comment, "I see my Long Island accent got you!"

At the Jamestown airport, as he prepared to leave, he addressed a large group of supporters. However, at the moment he began a criticism of Goldwater, his voice was drowned out by the roar of an airliner taking off. As the noise died Kennedy pointed to the rising jet and observed, "He's on his way back to Phoenix (Ariz.) to report!"

Accused of "carpetbagging" in his bid for New York's Senatorial seat, Robert Kennedy nevertheless won the election and later joked about the "carpetbag" issue at the 1965 Women's National Press Club Dinner: "I can't tell you how happy I am to be here representing the great state of...ah...ah...".

At one point in his campaign for the Senate seat from New York, Robert F. Kennedy observed, "I lived in New York for many years, but if this election is to be decided on the basis of who's lived here the longest, perhaps we should just elect the *oldest* man in the state."

Robert Kennedy was leafing through a promotional pamphlet that had been designed for his 1964 campaign, when he noticed a photograph of himself shaking hands with a notorious labor leader. He approached one of the advertising men handling his campaign and said, "There must be a better photo than this."

"What's wrong with this one?" asked the ad-man.

"That fellow's in jail," answered Kennedy.

A television network official was trying to smooth some ruffled feelings after an unfortunate incident at the studio during Robert F. Kennedy's 1964 campaign for the Senate. "We just try to do our best," said the official.

"That's all right," replied RFK. "We'll try to make up for your shortcomings."

Addressing the young people in one city on his 1964 campaign tour, Robert Kennedy said, "Back in the last town, I saw a sign that read, 'Respectable Young People for Keating.' Well, I don't know where that leaves *you*."

During his campaign rally in Riverhead, Long Island, candidate Robert Kennedy paused to count the number of Goldwater signs in the crowd. "One, two, three, four, five, six—I've been all up and down the state and that's the most Goldwater people I've seen in one place. I think they were flown in from Albany."

About to depart on one of his upstate swings in the 1964 Senatorial race, Robert Kennedy asked one reporter if he would be able to join the entourage. The reporter replied that he would be unable to come because he had previous commitments in Boston.

"Never heard of it," said Bobby.

In a 1964 campaign visit to the famed Grossinger's resort hotel in New York State, Robert F. Kennedy addressed a gathering of guests:

"The Catskills were immortalized by Washington Irving. He wrote of a man who fell asleep and awoke in another era. The only other area that can boast such a man is Phoenix, Arizona. . . . Barry Goldwater wants to give control of nuclear weapons to commanders in the field. Now that's my idea of high adventure. General Eisenhower says that he could *live* with a Goldwater Administration. Well, I suppose he'd have as good a chance as anyone else."

At Riverhead, Long Island, on one of Robert Kennedy's 1964 campaign stops, a young lad shouted to the candidate, "Go back where you came from!"

Kennedy, by this time an old hand at fielding these carpetbagger accusations, responded, "People have been telling me that all week—and that's why I'm here."

Senatorial candidate Robert F. Kennedy was a guest at a cocktail party attended by the political columnists for New York City's newspapers and magazines. During the evening one young woman came up to him and said, "I'm with the New York *Post,* and this is my first campaign."

"Mine too," answered Kennedy. "We'd better stay close together."

At the California Institute of Technology Robert Kennedy began a speech in a somewhat unorthodox way:

"Many of you, I know, are approaching the end of your schooling. The time of graduation — and liberation — is upon you. This is a time when you must expect to endure a good many profound remarks about your past and your future, your obligations and your challenges. I hesitate to afflict you further — and am consoled only by the fact that I went through a comparable ordeal when I finished college a few years back and I can recall not one word of what was said. This gives me, I might add, a pleasant sense of irresponsibility today."

Pasadena, California
June 8, 1964

During the 1964 Senatorial campaign (which ran concurrently with the Presidential campaign) Robert Kennedy put in an appearance on Barry Gray's New York radio discussion show. At one point Gray pointed out that his broadcast had quite a large audience, and Kennedy responded, "I always knew you had a large audience; everywhere I go in this state there's a group of people shouting, 'We want Barry.' "

Robert Kennedy resided in Brookline, Massachusetts, before he moved to Riverdale, New York, in 1964. However, during the campaign for the Senate he had occasion to explain, "Averell [Harriman] got that a little mixed up the other night. He introduced me at a Brooklyn rally as a local boy."

In the 1960 Presidential elections Teamster boss Jimmy Hoffa enlisted the support of his and several other unions against John F. Kennedy. Managing JFK's campaign was Robert F. Kennedy, who even then was an enemy of Hoffa, and who, as Attorney General, would eventually help put the union leader behind bars. Yet, when Joey Gallo, a notorious Brooklyn gangster, offered to use his power to help Bobby campaign for Jack, Bobby told him, "Just tell everybody you're voting for Nixon."

In April, 1968, while campaigning in California, Kennedy addressed a group of students at the beautiful Fresno State College. Looking around him at the verdant landscape, he joked about the hardships of going to college in such an idyllic setting:

"Just one sacrifice after another."

The advertising agency handling his 1964 Senatorial campaign informed Robert Kennedy that there were only three "fliers" in actual distribution, although another thirty-eight layouts were being prepared for circulation. Said Bobby, "Another week and you won't have to print anything. You can hand out the layouts."

There were allegations that Attorney General Robert Kennedy had decided to enter the 1964 Senatorial race at the behest of New York's "bosses." In one city, mobs of Kennedy-rooters crowded into the lobby of Kennedy's hotel, whereupon the candidate observed, "I am delighted to see so many *bosses* here to welcome me."

Candidate Robert Kennedy arrived several hours behind schedule for his campaign speech in Glens Falls, New York. Relieved to find the crowds still waiting for him, he expressed his gratitude for their patience, sighing, "Well, here we are five hours late. That's the well-oiled Kennedy machine for you."

By stapling new names over their old "Welcome Ted Kennedy" signs, economy-minded people in Massena, New York, succeeded in creating a perfectly passable bunch of "Welcome Bob Kennedy" signs for the candidate's 1964 campaign visit to their town. When Bobby noticed this phenomenon he tore his name off one sign and, showing it to the crowd, said, "There's one big advantage to electing me. It will be cheaper for everybody. We can interchange signs with Massachusetts."

During part of May, 1968, Senator Kennedy campaigned in Indiana. In Gary he began a speech with:

"I'm delighted to be here in Indiana. *In-dee-an-uh!* There was some fellow from Massachusetts here the other day who called it *In-dian-er*. That was my younger brother Teddy. He looks like me. But *I* call

it Indian-*uh!* And we're going to elect a President of the United States that knows how to pronounce the name of this state!"

During the controversial 1964 Senatorial campaign, Kennedy held several meetings with his staff concerning the meager assistance he was getting from the New York State Democratic Committee. Aware that he was not getting their unified financial support he finally said, "I guess I shouldn't complain. If they were any good, I wouldn't be here, would I?"

In an address given to the American Jewish Committee Appeal for Human Relations, Kennedy began with:

"I met this afternoon with members of the American Society of Newspaper Editors in Washington and we got along well, perhaps because some of them realized I used to be a newspaperman myself. I don't think I can lay claim to quite as close a bond at this gathering. Nonetheless, I am pleased and honored to join with you!"

New York City
April 16, 1964

While campaigning for the Democratic Presidential nomination Kennedy traveled across the nation. In April of 1968, while speaking to a crowd of native Nebraskans he grinned and said, "You may not know it, but I come from a farm state. New York is first in sour cherries."

In April, 1968, Senator Kennedy, seeking the Presidential nomination, campaigned through the Northwest by train. At one stop, while speaking from the observation platform, he noted some signs in the crowd being waved for another politician. Smiling, he said: "Actually Richard Nixon is speaking up in front of the train." He continued, "We thought that was only fair—he has no crowd at all."

In one of his first campaign speeches for the Democratic Presidential nomination, Kennedy alluded to the criticism he had received for seeking the nomination right after Eugene McCarthy's victory in the New Hampshire primary.

"Before I left Washington," he began, "I asked my younger brother, Teddy, to have 10,000 Kennedy campaign buttons made up. But when I opened them on the plane—I found they all had *his* picture on them."

As the audience began laughing he continued, "I told him it was too late to be getting into the campaign—besides that, it's downright ruthless."

While campaigning in California for the Democratic Presidential nomination, Senator Kennedy once addressed the student body at the San Fernando Valley State College. He was interrupted by the pealing of chimes. Pausing, he ad-libbed: "I'll get even with you, Ronald Reagan!"

Soon after announcing his candidacy for the Presidential nomination in 1968. Kennedy was asked by a reporter if this could advance his goals as Vice-President on a Johnson ticket.

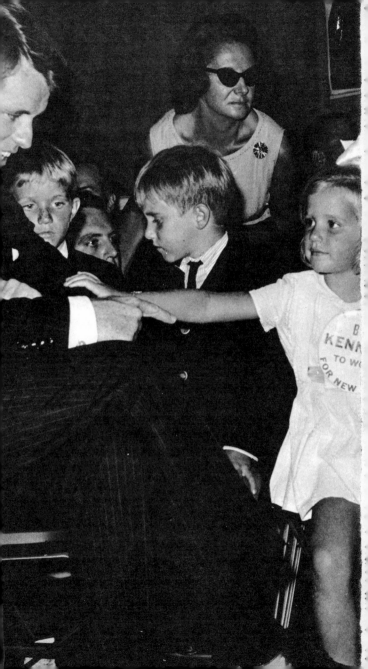

"No," Kennedy deadpanned, "and my feeling is that President Johnson wouldn't feel he could work toward his with me."

During the campaign for the Democratic Presidential nomination, Kennedy was addressing an audience in Nebraska when the wind tore a scrap of paper from his hand. He turned to an aide and quipped, "That's my farm program. Get it back quickly!"

During the campaigning for the 1968 Democratic Presidential nomination, Senator Kennedy was introduced to a crowd at the San Francisco airport by Mayor Doll who said, "I know God is on your side."
The Senator smiled and answered, "I only hope I have some delegates to go along with him."

Early in 1968 Senator Kennedy visited the offices of the Revitalization Corps, an organization started in honor of the late John F. Kennedy. He listened attentively to a taped interview with a very old man in Mississippi who had received aid from this organization. The elderly citizen spoke admiringly of the Senator and said on the recording, "I hope he gets to be Governor."
Said Kennedy, "I accept the nomination."

Kennedy, speaking before a student audience at the University of Pennsylvania in April, 1968, began with:

"I have a speech which it is my responsibility to give, and you have a responsibility to listen to it." He then added, "And if you finish before I do, let me know."

In April, 1968, after Johnson had declared that he would not run again for President, Senator Kennedy (who had declared himself in the campaign for the Democratic Presidential nomination) complained that he had lost his principal target. He remarked sadly, "I don't know what I can do now. It's no fun attacking Nixon so early in the game!"

During his campaign for the Presidential nomination, Senator Kennedy addressed a group of students at the University of Alabama. He began:

"I've had both some bad news and some good news since I got here. The bad news was that Bear Bryant (the University's football coach) will not run as my vice-president. The good news is that he's willing to let me run as his vice-president."

Robert Kennedy
as Attorney General and Senator

In a 1962 address before the American Booksellers Association, Attorney General Robert Kennedy was advocating the sharing of our technical publications with the developing countries abroad. He mentioned that there are many good Government Printing Office publications on government and history which might be useful abroad, and then said:

"Incidentally, we in the government are sometimes accused of being unimaginative. I am interested to find out that one of the GPO pamphlets on the technicalities of growing tomatoes is entitled, 'Hot Beds and Cold Frames.' *That* title should do well in *any* market."

A little boy in a Russian elementary school, when asked to describe the United States, said, "The United States is a sad country where workers and peasants are starving under capitalist exploitation by the cynical ruling classes."

"Correct," said the teacher, "and what is the major goal of the Soviet Union?"

"To catch up with the United States."

From a speech given in New York
January 22, 1963

Robert Kennedy was once asked his opinion of union leader Jimmy Hoffa's professed intent of organizing major league baseball players. His response: "I hope he doesn't get to first base."

Robert Kennedy told about one memorable visit on his trip to Rome:

"We had a friendly audience with Pope John. . . . He blessed us all, including the American newspapermen who were traveling with us, most of whom were not Catholics. He assured them that it was just a little blessing and wouldn't do them any harm."

The throngs that turned out for Robert Kennedy in Poland once delayed his arrival at a dinner. The Polish Communist officials were annoyed with Kennedy's "playing to the crowds," and rebuked him. "Premier Gomulka never does," they chided.

"Well," replied the exuberant Kennedy, "maybe *that's* the problem."

Attorney General Robert F. Kennedy was at a party for Abraham Ribicoff, who had recently resigned from his position as Secretary of Health, Education, and Welfare, in order to enter the race for Senator from Connecticut. Ribicoff said that he had found it difficult to maintain his image of being a moderate Democrat, because his Connecticut constituents associated him with Administration liberals such as Orville Freeman, Walter Heller, and Arthur Goldberg. At this point Kennedy put in, "Tell your people back home the President never has any Cabinet meetings and you've never even *met* any of those fellows."

James Bennett was the guest of honor at a Washington party celebrating his twenty-fifth year as chief of the federal prison system. He was in the process of slicing his large birthday cake when he

struck a hard object. After poking around in the cake for a moment, Bennett finally came up with the obstacle, an eight-inch file, hidden there by none other than Robert F. Kennedy.

During his official visit to Japan in 1962, Attorney General Robert Kennedy spoke at Nihon University, where, he later related, " . . . there were no heating facilities in the building but the university officials made arrangements to keep at least one part of us warm by placing electric cushions on our chairs. This can be slightly disconcerting, especially if it feels too warm and you can't find the switch to turn it off."

During the 1965 Mayoralty elections in New York City, Robert Kennedy was asked to campaign for Democratic candidate Abe Beame, who was losing some of the formerly Democratic neighborhoods in the city. In one such predominantly Irish neighborhood, Bobby exhorted the adults to return to the party of their fathers: "Don't you know we are all Democrats? We are the party of Roosevelt, Truman, Kennedy, Johnson, and . . ." Kennedy paused for a moment, scanning the multitude of Irish faces in the audience, and, smiling, concluded, ". . . Huey Long!"

In 1966, almost two full years after he had been elected as Senator from New York, Robert Kennedy received in the mail a form letter from Democratic National Chairman John Bailey. The letter had been forwarded from Kennedy's former voting

address, Barnstable, Massachusetts. The Senator mailed the letter back to Bailey with this note added:

"Dear John—I moved. Bob."

On one occasion Robert F. Kennedy was inspecting the Hudson River, notorious for its high level of pollution around New York City. Taking one sniff of a beaker of the fetid river water, Kennedy wrinkled up his nose and commented, "If you fall into this river, you won't drown—you'll decay!"

After he was elected Senator in the 1964 campaign, Robert Kennedy was invited to meet with the editorial staff of a New York City newspaper which had come out for Kenneth Keating and had, in fact, been highly critical of Kennedy's campaign. But Bobby broke up what might have been a grim meeting by opening with this remark: "First of all, I want to thank each and every one of you for your support!"

On one occasion Attorney General Robert F. Kennedy and Postmaster General J. Edward Day were addressing the same gathering, and Day happened to observe that half of the country's 35,000 postmasters were women. When the Attorney General rose to speak, he commenced: "It's all right about 50 per cent of Postmasters being women, but I think it is even more important that only 5 per cent of the inmates of our federal prisons are women."

Attorney General Robert Kennedy visited a Buddhist temple in Osaka during his trip to Japan

in 1962. When a priest gave him a stick of incense to burn, Kennedy turned to Ambassador Edwin O. Reischauer and asked if such a gesture would be appropriate. Reischauer informed him that it would merely be a demonstration of respect with no religious overtones, but Kennedy, a Roman Catholic, again asked, "You're sure it won't look as if I'm worshipping Buddha?"

The Ambassador reassured him that it was all right. Finally Kennedy gingerly picked up the stick of incense, and muttered to Reischauer under his breath, "If I get kicked out . . ."

While on a trip to Poland, Robert Kennedy drew big crowds wherever he went. In Cracow the crowds were particularly large and friendly. In passing, the Mayor asked him if he intended to run for President of the United States. Looking over the crowd, Kennedy replied, "No, I don't think I'll run for President. I think I'll run for Mayor of Cracow!"

In 1967 Robert Kennedy addressed the Gridiron Club in Washington as spokesman for the Democratic party. Governor Reagan spoke for the Republicans. Alluding to his less-than-amicable relationship with President Johnson, Senator Kennedy began by addressing the Gridiron's president as: "Mr. President—the friendliest president in town."

He then turned to Reagan, and referred to him as: "the *acting* Governor of California."

Arriving late at a Business Council Meeting in Washington, Attorney General Robert Kennedy

apologized and said that he owed his tardiness to "a suit filed by the Dupont Company to require the Justice Department to divest itself of the Anti-trust Division."

At the time when Senator Robert Kennedy announced his proposal that the Viet Cong comprise a part of the peacetime government of Vietnam, Vice-President Humphrey was visiting that embattled country. As the controversial proposal made news, Humphrey commented that Kennedy's idea "was like putting a fox in the chicken coop."

But when the Vice-President returned to Washington he found this tension-relieving letter from Bobby on his desk:

Dear Hubert,

Welcome home. I was taking care of everything back here while you were away. Perhaps you heard. As a matter of fact, I felt a little like a fox in the chicken house myself.

Congratulations on your trip.

Best, Bob.

Before R.F.K. announced for the Presidency, one of his more enthusiastic boosters wrote him a letter in which, certain that Kennedy was sure to be President one day, he asked for an advance copy of his Inaugural Address. Seizing the opportunity to rib the Vice-President, Bobby sent the letter to Humphrey along with this note: "Dear Mr. Vice-President. I thought you would like to see a typical sample of my mail. . . . Bob."

In August, 1965, Senator Robert Kennedy was concluding some remarks honoring forty-three graduates of a VISTA training program. One of the trainees suggested that Kennedy officially swear them in, whereupon Kennedy, finding out that there was no official oath, made up his own: "Repeat after me. I swear that I will be a good VISTA volunteer. I will assist those in need, help my U.S. Senator all I can, and otherwise behave myself. So help me God."

Following the Democratic Nominating Convention of 1964, the Robert Kennedys were planning to hold a large and festive reception for the delegates. Every last detail of the arrangements was carefully attended to, with the exception of the mailing of the delegates' invitations. When the grievous oversight was discovered, "Kennedy hostesses" began to invite random passersby in to fill up the party. When Bobby Kennedy finally learned of the error, he nodded his head and quipped, "I knew there was something wrong. Not enough people were wearing delegate badges, and too many were carrying boxes marked Macy's."

During his 1965 tour of several South American countries, Robert Kennedy decided to cool off and get some exercise by taking a swim alongside the Indian canoe in which he had been traveling. Suddenly the Senator looked up and, mimicking the hearty baritone of a news commentator, announced: "It was impossible to pinpoint the time when he decided to run for President, but the idea seemed to take hold as he was swimming in the Amazonian river of Nhamunda, keeping an eye out for the man-eating piranhas."

Then he paused for a moment, reflecting, and added, "Piranhas have never been known to bite a U.S. Senator."

Speaking before the 1966 luncheon for the Federation of Jewish Philanthropies, Senator Robert Kennedy found himself following the famous lawyer and eloquent speaker, Louis Nizer. Kennedy used this analogy to convey his feelings about such a situation: "A man bored everyone he met by relating his experiences during the Johnstown flood. . . . When he died, he asked Saint Peter to gather an audience so that he could tell them his story of the Johnstown flood. Saint Peter agreed, but warned him: 'Remember, Noah will be in the audience.' "

Seeing that President Johnson's "Great Society" concept had become a byword on the nation's lips, New York's Governor Nelson Rockefeller decided to adopt the "Just Society" as a catchy slogan for his 1966 re-election campaign. Taking due note of this phenomenon in an address before a Democratic meeting in Albany, Senator Robert Kennedy took the trend to its logical conclusion: "What we really need, gentlemen," advised Bobby, "is a *Just Great* Society."

As a newly elected Senator from New York, Robert F. Kennedy was near the bottom of the priority list for Senate seats. Remarked Bobby, "I had better seats for *Hello, Dolly!*"

As a sportsman, Senator Robert Kennedy enjoyed himself when he addressed the 1965 edition of the Baseball Writers' dinner:

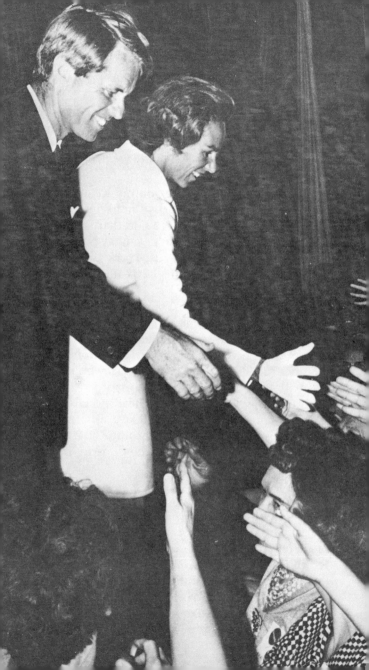

"I can't believe all those things Ted Williams says about you fellows are true.

"Since my election, I've received many invitations for speaking engagements—from the Overseas Press Club to the Puerto Rican forum. It seems they want me to speak everywhere but on the floor of the Senate.

"I am delighted to see Johnny Keane here tonight—he's new to New York—I'm his guide.

"One of the writers here said that last November I stole home and it wasn't even my home. Being originally from Massachusetts, I was automatically a Yankee. But during the last campaign, I kept hearing, 'Yankee go home.'

"I'm also glad to see Yogi Berra here. I understand he is writing a book: *Lucky to be a Yankee*. By Yogi Berra, as told to Mel Allen.

"I've also been talking to Joe Cronin. I remember in 1961, when Dave Powers, who is a great baseball fan, brought Joe Cronin into President Kennedy's office to present the traditional baseball pass. President Kennedy said, 'Dave, what was that story you told me about Joe Cronin?'

"Dave looked at Cronin and said, 'Lifetime average of .302?'

"The President said, 'No.'

" 'Hall of Fame?'

"The President said, 'No.'

" 'Mr. President, you must mean the time Carl Hubbell struck out five Hall of Famers in a row—Ruth, Gehrig, Foxx, Simmons, and Joe Cronin.'

" 'Yes, that's the story.'

"And Joe said, 'Mr. President, it's a pleasure to strike out in such company.'

"I enjoy baseball, and I found last year's pennant races very exciting. In the National League they couldn't decide who the leader was until the very last day. It sounds like the New York Legislature.

"A number of people here have asked me about that situation. I want to make it clear that there is no truth to reports that I am manager of the Albany Democrats.

"What they're doing up there reminds me of the time when Wilbert Robinson was managing the Brooklyn Dodgers, and three of them arrived at third base at the same time. They asked Uncle Robbie whether he was upset. He said, 'Hell, no, that's the closest those fellows have been to each other all season.'

"I have nine children now—enough for a baseball team. We'll be training soon. Maybe Frank Lane will buy us.

"With all these children I've decided to run my house like the Senate. We have a new speaker. We're working on a Medicare program. But the rest of the family doesn't seem to want to follow the seniority rule.

"The other day a bell rang and I got ready to go to vote. But Ethel said it was just the signal for the four o'clock feeding. . . .

"Speaking seriously, baseball has been our national sport for almost a hundred years. Other sports may be faster, or more exciting on television, but baseball is much more than a spectator sport. When you go out on a nice day, in every playground and vacant lot you will find them playing baseball. It is a part of every man's life. It is a part of our country and will continue to be. As Grantland Rice once said, 'From one ole cat to the last at bat.'

"Some say that baseball is on the way down. But as long as young boys have heroes, and as long as the players and owners and all of you meet your responsibilities, I think baseball is on the way up.

"Finally, let me say that I did not run for the Senate to become Commissioner of Baseball. I'm not interested in the position because it doesn't have enough power."

Robert Kennedy decided to take some time off for a skiing trip in 1964. But when a visitor to his office told Kennedy that he was glad he was getting away, Bobby said, "You're the ninth person to tell me that today. What's everybody plotting here, a palace coup?"

Addressing the Linn County Veterans' Council during the 1962 Veterans' Day program at Albany, Oregon, Attorney General Robert Kennedy remarked:

"Sometimes I think every resident of your State is a self-appointed missionary to convert misguided Easterners who say 'Ore-gonn.'

"Perhaps the best job ever done along this line was by L. H. Gregory, the widely known sports editor of the *Oregonian*. Some years ago, he told a Texas audience that he, too, greatly appreciated their hospitality to him, but that if they persisted in pronouncing Oregon with the accent on the last syllable, he would have to start accenting Texas in the same way."

Attorney General Robert Kennedy addressed the Commencement Exercises at Manhattan College in

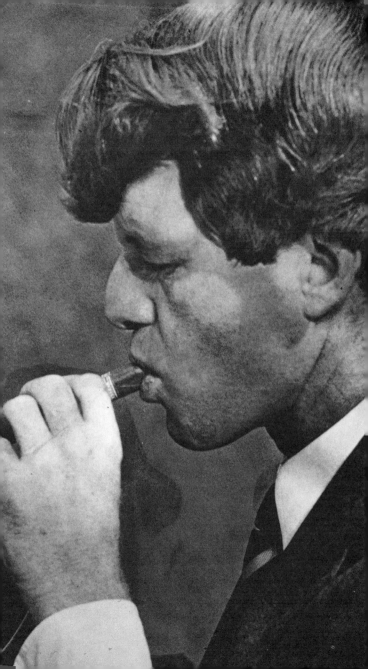

New York City on June 12, 1962. After receiving an honorary degree the Attorney General commented:

"To receive this recognition without the normal academic niceties of attendance, absorption and exams—not to mention tuition—does not really detract too much from the pleasure of the award. In fact, I most strongly advocate the merit system now in vogue at Manhattan College.

"I could, I know, express this simple word of thanks and subside into silence, to the accompaniment of your grateful sighs of relief. I agree that the commencement exercises at all colleges should be an elective. The long elocution lavished on captive graduates represents the final on-campus sacrifice you will be constrained to offer up for some worthy intention.

"A truly Christian Brother briefed me on the ground rules of your more recent commencements. He actually used the word 'brief.' He alluded delicately to the 1888 graduation when the visiting archbishop of San Luis Potosí was called upon merely to give a final blessing to Cardinal Hayes' graduating class. He spoke ornately, and occasionally in English, for almost *two* hours.

"On these otherwise glad occasions, pundits in possession of the podium are tempted, by tradition, to reveal the accumulated wisdom of a long and mature experience. For me, this is rather easy; but as Brother A. Joseph, my mentor, discreetly hinted, even seniors seldom learn from second-hand experience—and never do on commencement day.

"Yet paradoxically, in connection with this very occasion, I, myself, have learned a lot from experience—the experience and history of your college. 159 pages. . . ."

Kennedy then went on to trace the founding and growth of the Catholic institution:

"The cunning Christian Brothers, real estate experts, bought the wrong sites three times, the back of the old college became the front, new stories were added to old buildings at the bottom and the college was sold for taxes once.

"It has had at times classrooms and no students and at other times students without classrooms.

"I mention these four things not to suggest that miscalculations are not confined to Washington, to any political party or era but rather as dramatic proof of what basic unity, solidarity, loyalty, good will and a sense of sacrifice could do against handicaps and great odds in a world beyond Manhattan."

Speaking before a group of foreign correspondents in Tokyo during his 1962 visit to Japan, Robert Kennedy said: "I had seaweed for breakfast yesterday. To tell you the honest-to-goodness truth, it didn't taste bad. When I went to Central Asia with Justice Douglas in 1955, they brought in a goat, very dead, plucked out its eyes, and served them to us. Justice Douglas turned to me and said, 'For the sake of America, Bob, make like it's an oyster!' So things have gone up since then."

Recalled Kennedy about his visit to Japan, "It did seem embarrassing to me to come to the end of a meeting with the Foreign Minister of Japan and then suddenly thrust on him an autographed photograph of myself. I could imagine his sick smile as he opened it and said, 'Just what I *always* wanted.'"

"When I gave the picture to one of the ministers, I told him that at least it was a nice frame and that he could take my picture out and replace it with one of his wife. He laughed—slightly nervous, I thought—as if I had read his own thoughts."

In September, 1962, Attorney General Robert F. Kennedy spoke at the dedication of Kendrick Hall at the University of San Francisco Law School. He began:

". . . I am aware that you have spent two long days now celebrating your law school's golden anniversary. I suspect that the greatest virtue in any more oratory will be in its blessed brevity. If I had any doubts on this score, Father Callahan's letter of invitation delicately enlightened me. He mentioned that Father Connoly was recovering from a spinal disk operation and also that the affair did not have to last too long. I am not clear whether he was whispering a hint, a hope or a prayer. You can never be sure with Father Callahan. But I'll try to keep in mind that any old place in a speech is a wonderful place to stop. I would not want any speech-induced discomfort of Father Connoly to become a widespread affliction of this assemblage."

Robert Kennedy was a hard-working public official, his duties occasionally claiming his time even on holidays. One Washington's Birthday during his Attorney Generalship, Kennedy noticed a few automobiles parked in the Justices' parking spots and took down their license numbers so that he could write each one of them a letter of commendation. Unexpectedly, one wrote back, "I cannot tell a lie on Washington's Birthday—I used my parking space but I went to the movies."

Replied Kennedy, "With honesty like yours, our country's cherry trees are safe."

In 1962 Attorney General Robert F. Kennedy spoke before the annual luncheon of the Associated Press, and began:

"There have been some comments about the Department of Justice awakening three newsmen in the middle of the night to ask some questions. I want to tell you the reaction of your reporter, Louis Panos, who covers the Department of Justice for the Associated Press. The next evening Mr. Panos came into my office and said, 'I am just leaving for home and before I go to bed is there anything you'd really like to know?' Then he said, 'Don't call me. *I'll* call *you.*'

"I want to assure you that we do not make a practice of calling reporters at two or three o'clock in the morning. But, to tell the truth, when *I* get called at two or three in the morning by a reporter from the Associated Press—and it happens—I am not too sure it wouldn't be a good idea!"

The subject of that speech was foreign misinformation and misunderstanding about the United States. To illustrate his point, Kennedy told this anecdote:

". . . It was not just with the students that I encountered this misinformation. The head of a leading Japanese labor organization with millions of members told me that a few industrialists—Wall Street, the Morgan Bank and the Rockefellers—run the United States. I said, 'Not yet!' "

Robert Kennedy was often so intently wrapped up in his work that he was absent-minded about "details" he couldn't be bothered with. Once he went to a parking lot to pick up his car, a Mercury station wagon he had been driving for months. After he rummaged through his pockets for a while looking for the ticket, the parking attendant finally asked, "What kind of car?"

"Oh," replied Bobby vaguely, "it's a Ford or Chevrolet or one of that kind."

At the height of the civil rights disturbances in Oxford, Mississippi, in 1962, Attorney General Robert Kennedy received a telephone call from an aide who reported that the embattled Justice Department officers at the university campus felt like the defenders of the Alamo. "Well," Kennedy reminded the aide, "you know what happened to *those* guys."

In October of 1966 Robert Kennedy flew to California to address the student body at the University of California at Berkeley. At that time the students at Berkeley had been making headlines because of their political militancy. Said Kennedy:

"You are the first college to become a major political issue since George III attacked Harvard for being a center of rebellion and subversion. And —he was right!"

In March, 1968, Senator Robert Kennedy addressed a large audience at Kansas State University in Man-

hattan, Kansas. Alluding to his ties to both Boston and New York, Kennedy began:

"The reason I'm here is that someone sent me a history of this city. And I found out that it was founded by people from Chicago who came to Kansas to found a town named Boston which they later changed to Manhattan. So I knew I'd be right at home!"

A reporter traveling with Kennedy and an aide noticed that the briefcases of both men were identical. She asked, "What happens if you get them mixed up?" Kennedy's reply was, "Mine's full of dirty laundry so it doesn't matter!"

In March, 1965, Bobby Kennedy and the National Geographic Society party reached the summit of the mountain peak to be then named Mt. Kennedy. On the way up he and his friend Jim Whittaker were making good time when Whittaker asked him, "How did you practice for the climb? What exercises did you do?"

Kennedy replied, "Well, I practiced *yells*. Yells like 'Help!' and 'Pull me up!' and other ones like that."

"There's an acid joke about the Negro who attempted to register in a southern county. The registrar asked him to copy and interpret the 14th Amendment. He did so, brilliantly. 'All right, if you're so smart,' the registrar said, 'recite the Gettysburg Address from memory.' The Negro did. 'Okay, give us the Second Inaugural speech.' Again the Negro came through beautifully. Finally, the registrar pulled a Chinese newspaper out of his desk and asked, 'Can you read this?' 'That's easy,' said the black man. 'It says, 'No Negroes are going to vote in *this* state this year.' "

> *Speech before the*
> *Civil Rights Committee*
> *New York City Central Labor Council*
> *AFL-CIO*
> *New York City*
> *March 9, 1963*

"There is, of course, freedom in the USSR to say the right thing. This was brought home to a young American visitor to Moscow who was earnestly explaining how any American could openly denounce the life and morality of the United States —even ridicule the President.

" 'It is the same here,' said the guide. 'A Soviet citizen may also denounce life and morality in the United States and ridicule your President.' "

> *From a speech delivered in*
> *New York City*
> *January 22, 1963*

"When Mr. Khrushchev reported that the Cosmonauts—like the Bolshevik pilots of the early twenties—reported seeing 'no signs of God,' we can only suggest that they aim—with the rest of mankind—a little higher."

> *From an address to the*
> *Center for Study of Democratic Institutions*
> *of the Fund for the Republic*
> *New York City*
> *January 22, 1963*

One day, when Attorney General, Kennedy assembled his top aides together and told them he would be away from the Justice Department for a short time. "It would be terrible," he concluded, "if the Department *improves* while I'm gone."

During a question and answer period following a speech to a college audience, a student pressed Kennedy doggedly about his days as an aide to Senator Joseph McCarthy. At one point Kennedy's notes slipped off the rostrum and, bending down, he said, "I'm not disappearing. I'm just picking up my notes."

A biographer of John F. Kennedy once wrote that Robert Kennedy was anti-Semitic. The Attorney General's press secretary Ed Guthman, who is Jewish, brought the book to his boss and showed him the passage. After reading it, Kennedy looked up and stared hard at Guthman. "I always knew," he said, deadpan, "there was something about you I hated."

"Thomas Jefferson once said that he cared not who made a country's laws, so long as he could write its newspapers. If this Congress goes on much longer, I'd rather be in the newspaper business, too."

From a speech delivered in New York City October 9, 1965

While Attorney General, Robert Kennedy told a group of young lawyers on his staff who were visiting his office:

"After all, I came to this department ten years ago as an assistant attorney making $4,200 a year. But I had ability and integrity, an interest in my work. I stayed late hours, my brother became President, and now I'm Attorney General." Pause. "Those qualifications were not necessarily listed in their order of importance."

A week after his March, 1968, speech on Vietnam in which he criticized the Johnson administration, Senator Kennedy told a banquet audience, "I had a nice meeting with the President this week. We talked about a cease-fire, escalation, and prospects of negotiations for peace." He paused. "And he said when I come back next time we might talk about Vietnam."

Senator Kennedy once announced he had received a crucial telegram from Teddy:

"President is in Asia. Vice-President is in midwest. You are in Michigan. Have seized control.

Teddy"

G. Mennen Williams, whom John F. Kennedy had appointed Undersecretary of State for African Affairs, and Robert Kennedy toured Africa together and when they returned, Bobby reported that "Soapy" had done quite a job. Said Kennedy,

"Everyplace we went the natives ran up wearing a loincloth and a bow tie and shouting, 'Vote Democratic.'"

Senator Kennedy's campaigns had always attracted youthful and enthusiastic supporters. Looking over one audience that seemed filled with some very young admirers, he commented:

"I'm going to lower the voting age to—seven."

Appearing with Robert Kennedy on the *Tonight* show were the rock 'n' roll singers, the Righteous Brothers. After the show they invited Senator Kennedy to join them for dinner, but couldn't remember the name of the place they wanted to go to—just that you couldn't smoke or drink there. Kennedy finally remarked, "You must mean Horn and Hardart's!"

During the 1966 Congressional hearings on automobile safety Robert Kennedy gave an example of his sometimes bitingly sarcastic wit. Never one to defer to older politicians only because they were older, Kennedy vented his wrath at Senator Carl Curtis for preventing Ralph Nader, an outspoken critic of the car industry, from offering his complete testimony. "What I don't understand," Kennedy began, "is why you don't let Mr. Nader read his statement to find out if in fact—"

"I have no objection to his reading his statement," interrupted Curtis.

"Then maybe we would understand his position," continued Kennedy. "I don't know how you can reach a conclusion about his position. First, you admit you haven't read his book; and secondly, you haven't heard his testimony. Why don't you listen to his testimony and then criticize?"

"I have no objection to hearing his testimony," Curtis again asserted, "but when he loses me with—"

"With big words?" queried Kennedy.

In 1962 Attorney General Robert Kennedy's office was in charge of soliciting contributions from American businessmen for the liberation of Castro's prisoners from Cuba. As Kennedy tells it, some business leaders made contributions out of humanitarian ideals, some because they knew the donations would be tax-deductible anyway, and others "perhaps felt they'd like to have a warmer relationship with the Government."

At one stop on a trip to Korea, Robert Kennedy received a short briefing from a certain Army general. Later Kennedy said to a friend, "I don't want to worry you. But you remember that general who explained how we would handle the North Koreans if they attacked? Well, the last time I saw him was two years ago in Berlin when he told us what we would do if the Russians ever moved in on us there. The only other time I saw him was when he was holding a briefing on the Bay of Pigs Operation."

Invited to speak at the Seattle World's Fair in August, 1962, Robert Kennedy opened his remarks by saying:

"I have waited a long time for this visit to the Pacific Northwest. Mr. Justice Douglas has often assured me that this is the most beautiful and exciting part of the United States, and, as a mere Attorney General, who am I to argue against the Supreme Court?

"Moreover, there are, I believe, about as many graduates of the University of Washington in Washington, D.C., as graduates of Harvard—and they are worse than Texans in their enthusiasm for their native state."

The Family

In some of his addresses as Attorney General, Robert Kennedy enjoyed telling this anecdote about the time he was talking to a certain businessman:

"I don't trust your brother," the businessman scolded.

"My brother, the President?" asked Kennedy.

"No, your brother, Ted," was the reply. "And furthermore, you're listening too much to Arthur."

"Arthur Schlesinger?" suggested Bobby.

"No, Arthur Goldberg," answered the businessman. "What's more, you should take more advice from Rose."

"Alex Rose, the New York Liberal Party leader?"

"No, your mother, Rose," the businessman said.

At one stop on Robert Kennedy's 1964 campaign tour both he and his wife were surrounded by autograph seekers. After a while Robert was able to free himself and make his way to the waiting car, but Ethel remained behind to sign autographs. "Ethel," implored Bobby, finally, "Ethel, *I'm* the candidate."

In 1966 Senator Robert Kennedy, then the father of nine, received a letter from a seven-year-old Farmingdale, Long Island, boy who asked, "Do you take good care of your children?"

The Senator decided that the issue was worth sharing with the rest of his constituents, so in his September newsletter he quoted the little boy's query and replied: "I asked my children and they voted 'yes' by 4 to 3 with 2 abstentions."

During the 1964 Senatorial campaign, Robert Kennedy was accused by many of being a "carpetbagger." He had only lived in New York State as a child and had always been considered, along with all the other Kennedys, as a resident of Massachusetts. However, Kennedy learned to field these accusations well. When a youngster asked Robert Kennedy why he had left Riverdale, New York, as a child, Kennedy answered:

"I didn't want to leave. I was seven years old at the time and I pleaded with my mother, 'Why must we leave Riverdale?' But we left anyway."

Near the time when Senator Kennedy was to declare himself in the race for Democratic Presidential nomination, he addressed a group of businessmen. He told them that the only reason he was reassessing his political plans was because "I ordered 40 balloons for my children and they sent me 40,000."

In March, 1968, Senator Kennedy addressed a group of students at Brigham Young University in Provo, Utah. He opened with the remark that he and his wife "spent part of our honeymoon here and have had ten children since, so I guess I learned something!"

While campaigning for the 1968 Democratic Presidential campaign, Senator Kennedy traveled and spoke tirelessly through Indiana. Later he said jokingly that the Indiana campaign had "aged" him.

He commented that someone there had told him it was nice of him to bring his daughter along, "And they were talking about my wife, Ethel."

Robert Kennedy was gravely troubled over accepting the post of Attorney General under his brother's Administration. In one telephone conversation with President Kennedy early in 1961, he alluded to a much publicized Eisenhower defense of Sherman Adams, apropos of his own situation: "Why don't you say I may be your brother, but you need me?"

In January, 1963, a newsman asked Robert Kennedy if having a brother who was President were not a problem for him at times. Replied the Attorney General, *"I* don't find it so. It might be for him, but it isn't for me."

When Robert F. Kennedy formally declared his intention to strive for the 1964 Democratic candidacy for United States Senator, a newsman asked him if this was the first time he had ever run for public office. Smiled Kennedy, "Yes, but I've had a couple of relatives who did."

While campaigning in April, 1968, Kennedy had a whistle-stop tour of the Northwest. Stopping in Columbus, Nebraska, Kennedy began his speech from the platform by gesturing toward Ethel and saying, "Now you wouldn't want her to have to say, 'He lost in Nebraska.' A nice girl like that—with all those children."

During his visit to Tokyo in 1962, Attorney General Robert Kennedy related this story: "A man asked for a judgeship for his brother. I declined— and I received the inevitable phone call. He said, 'After all, your brother appointed you Attorney General.'

"I answered, 'We only serve the will of the President.' "

Speaking before the 1961 "Dinner of Champions" in New York City, Attorney General Robert F. Kennedy remarked:

"Standing here, surrounded by so many athletes, I feel I ought to present my credentials. I come from a family that has always emphasized and enjoyed sports—golf, tennis, football, baseball, and the rest. Last year, for instance, we did considerable running. So I come naturally by my interest in sports."

One of the commonest charges leveled at Robert Kennedy during his 1964 Senatorial race was that he was the bosses' choice. Countered Kennedy, "I have only one boss and she's at home."

A woman in Saranac, New York, once boarded the Kennedy family's private plane by mistake, and was taken aback to find therein Mrs. John F. Kennedy, Robert Kennedy, and a number of assorted children. "She was a very nice woman," said Robert later, "but she thought it was very crowded for a commercial plane."

". . . They have told me when you speak in Georgia you should try to tie yourself to Georgia and the South, and even better, claim some Georgia kinfolk. There are a lot of Kennedys in Georgia. But as far as I can tell, I have no relatives here and no direct ties to Georgia, except one. This State gave my brother the biggest percentage majority of any state in the union and in this last election that was even *better* than kinfolk!"

Law Day Exercises of the
University of Georgia Law School
May 6, 1961

On the day that John F. Kennedy was elected President in 1960, the family played a spirited game of touch football on the lawn of their Hyannis Port home. Bobby was playing quarterback, while Jack played end. On one play Jack moved downfield for a pass. In the clear for a moment, Jack reached up for the ball, but as the defense closed in on him, he dropped it. Observed the quarterback, Bobby, "That's my brother. All guts, no brains."

People were always concerned about the relationship of Robert Kennedy and his brother, Jack, when Jack was in the White House. Robert remarked that many people seemed to overlook the fact that the two men had been closely allied long before Jack became President. Stated Bobby in January, 1963, "I've been associated with the present incumbent in the White House for thirty-seven years, the first few of which were slow."

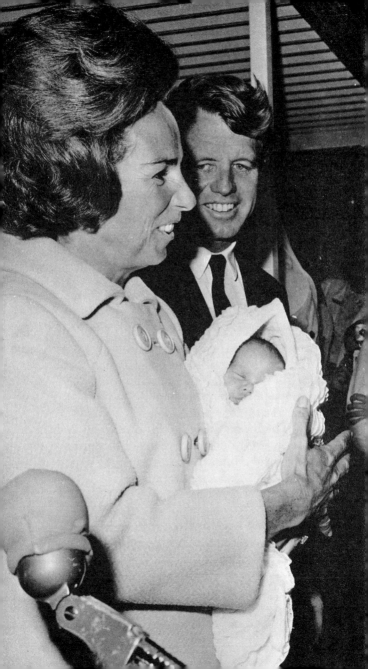

The popular Kennedy family campaigns as a unit when any of its members are involved in a political contest. Robert Kennedy, as well as his mother, wife, brother and sisters campaigned vigorously for his brother John in all of his political races. Robert is credited with this concise speech at one rally during John's 1952 Senatorial campaign against Henry Cabot Lodge:

"My brother Jack couldn't be here. My mother couldn't be here. My sister Eunice couldn't be here, my sister Pat couldn't be here, my sister Jean couldn't be here, but if my brother Jack *were* here he'd tell you Lodge has a very bad voting record."

Organizing the entire Robert F. Kennedy family for an outing of any kind was a formidable problem in logistics. On one occasion Bobby lined up his nine children and told them, "We're all going to a convention—now be good. I have something for the one who's best."

The brood turned to file out, when their father added, "And one more thing—I'll *also* have something for the one who's worst."

In 1965 Senator Robert Kennedy addressed the International Radio and Television Society on the subject of foreign aid, advocating assistance in "programs of family planning" for foreign nations who requested it. Suddenly Kennedy, himself the father of nine children, stopped, turned to his wife, and said, "You'd better leave."

During the Senate Foreign Relations Committee hearings early in 1966, Senator Robert Kennedy became increasingly concerned that the issue of what role—if any—the Viet Cong would play in Vietnamese peace talks was being avoided. He put his staff of speechwriters to work on a statement of his position on that issue, and delivered his unsolicited minority opinion at a well-covered press conference the next day. When one reporter asked him what he planned to do next with his proposals, Kennedy smiled and shrugged, "I guess I'll take them home and show them to my wife."

Early in 1963 Attorney General Robert Kennedy was mistakenly given a telephone call for "Senator Kennedy." Commented Bobby, "That's how it goes. First they mistook me for Jack, and now, Teddy."

At one campaign stop in 1964 Robert Kennedy opened his speech with these remarks: "A few months ago I was having breakfast with my wife. And I was reading in the papers that California had replaced New York as the number-one state in population—so I turned to my wife and I said, 'What can we *do*?' So I moved to New York, and in just one day I increased the population by ten and a half —my opponent has just sixty days to match that record."

Speaking before the Foreign Student Service Council, Robert Kennedy became a little tongue-

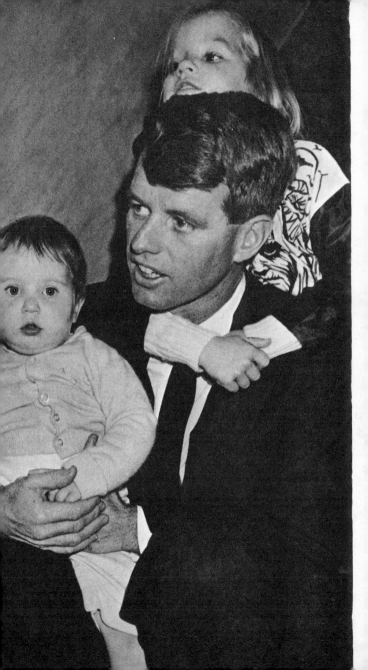

tied while trying to pronounce one of his brother's most memorable sentences: "You people are exemplifying what my brother meant when he said in his inaugural address, 'Ask what you can do for—uh—uh—do not ask what you can do—uh—ask not what you can do for your country but—' Well, anyhow, you remember his words."

As the audience broke into laughter, Bobby went on: "That's why my *brother* is President."

A good deal of talk has been made of the Kennedy millions. But Robert Kennedy was capable of treating this subject, like almost any other, with great irony. RFK once spoke with an author who was writing a book about him, and asked the writer how he looked in the book. Replied the writer, "Like a million dollars." Said Bobby, "That's awfully low for a Kennedy."

John F. Kennedy was a runaway winner in his 1960 Presidential primary race in West Virginia. At a celebration following the closing of the polls, Ethel Kennedy went around snapping pictures and exclaiming, "Isn't it exciting?" Confessed the blasé Robert Kennedy to reporters, "I couldn't have done it without my brother."

Reputed to be an extremely ambitious politician, Senator Robert F. Kennedy made this announcement at the Women's National Press Club dinner for the new Congress in 1965: "I want to assure you I have no Presidential aspirations—nor does my wife, Ethel Bird."

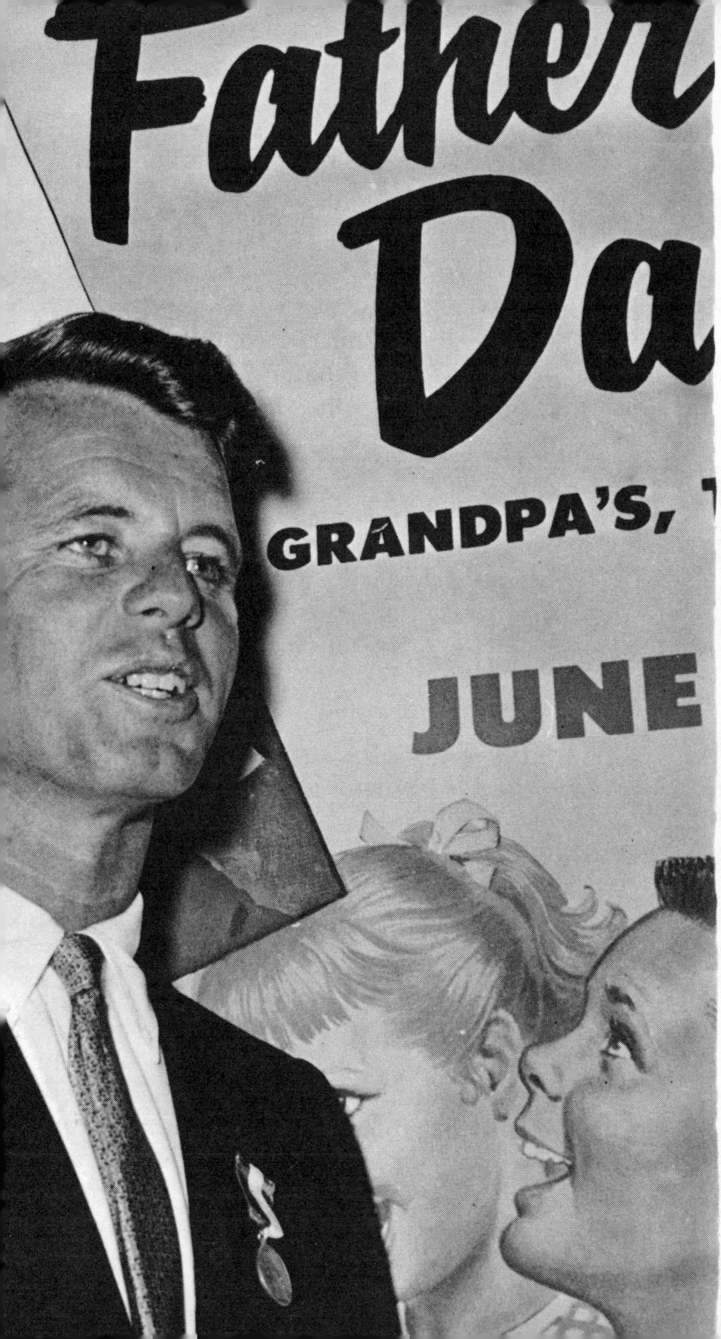
Father
Da
GRANDPA'S,
JUNE

Once Bobby Kennedy's young daughter Kerry rushed up to him, threw her arms around him and gave him a loving kiss on the cheek. Said Bobby, teasingly, "Please Kerry, I told you—only when there are cameramen around."

A lawyer in the Justice Department was discussing a certain business that was allowed to deteriorate by the founder's son, when the then Attorney General Robert Kennedy remarked, "That's one mistake *our* father never made—taking us into business with him."

As one particularly passionate campaign speech during the spring of 1968 drew to a close, Kennedy paused, then wrapped up his pitch for the vote by closing, "Think of all those little children whose father might be unemployed!"

At his 1964 Senatorial campaign debut at New York's Fulton Fish Market, Robert Kennedy promised, "I have eight children, and we eat fish every Friday. From now on, we'll eat fish *twice* a week. That's what we're going to do for the fishing industry of New York."

When Robert Kennedy had finished his address to the students of Waseda University in Japan, a young cheerleader came forward to lead the students in their school song. As Bobby himself tells it, "During the first chorus he accidentally struck my wife in the pit of the stomach. She said it didn't hurt, or at least not nearly so much as it would have if he hadn't been a friend."

Robert Kennedy's quips were often at his own expense. The following example took place with a visitor at his home not long after he had declared himself a candidate for the Democratic Presidential nomination. It was also not long after one of his oldest friends, Averell Harriman, had announced his support of President Johnson. When presenting his youngest child to the visitor he said:

"This is Douglas Harriman Kennedy. The middle name is, of course, for one of my hard-core supporters, Averell Harriman!"

At dinner one night at the home of the Robert Kennedys, a reporter noticed the absence of any children.

"Where did you hide the kids?" he asked.

"What kids?" replied Kennedy, deadpan.

"We only have them to get in the papers," Ethel whispered. *"Then* we farm them out."

A reporter once asked Robert Kennedy whether the death of his two brothers, Joe Jr. and John, and the near-death of the third, Ted, after an airplane crash, had affected his religious beliefs. He replied immediately, "No, they do not." Then he smiled and added, "Of course, we do occasionally think that someone up in heaven is out to lunch when he ought to be attending to business."

When on vacation one summer and out boating, a Coast Guard boat raced to Senator Kennedy to inform him that his son Bob, Jr., had injured his foot by cutting it on glass. When he arrived back home his son was in fine shape but with one foot in

a cast. Relieved and with a smile, Kennedy wrote on the sole of his other foot, "Next time don't ruin my vacation. Keep *this* foot *out* of the glass."

Robert Kennedy had ten children and he often joked about the size of his family. While in South Dakota during his campaign in May, 1968, he said:

"The head of the World Population Control Council thinks I would be a bad influence in the White House!"

During the 1968 campaign for the Democratic Presidential nomination, Senator Kennedy spoke in Columbus, Indiana. He began one speech by reporting:

"We took a poll among my children. We wanted a cross-section of whom the young generation wanted for President. *I* got four votes. Two votes went to my brother Teddy. Two went to my sister Pat. The others are reassessing their position."

Prior to 1960 Mrs. Arthur Schlesinger, Jr. was a staunch supporter of Adlai Stevenson, to the vexation of her husband. Confronting Mr. Schlesinger with this fact, Robert Kennedy once asked, "Can't you control your own wife, or are you like me?"

While Attorney General, Kennedy's office was filled with photographs of his large family. One prominent photograph was of his son David on the White House lawn. A visitor once paused to read the inscription President Kennedy had scrawled on the photo. Kennedy picked it up and read it aloud,

"A future president inspects his property." Then, with a smile, he said, "That *proves* there's a dynasty!"

Ethel Kennedy, to her surprise, won the Homemaker of the Year award in 1958. When asked if her husband was pleased, she replied, "Oh yes, but he said I had better hurry down and get the prize before someone sees the house."

Bobby was considered the "toughest" of the Kennedy sons—in spite of, or perhaps because of, his smaller stature. He once noted:

"I was the seventh of nine children. And when you come from *that* far down, you have to struggle to survive."

Speaking at a dinner in Philadelphia for the Americans for Democratic Action, Kennedy spotted Congressman William Green in the audience. Green's father had been a big political boss in the tradition the ADA was created to oppose. "Billy," said Kennedy, "how would your father feel if he knew you were here?" Then he paused, "Come to think of it—how would *my* father feel if he knew *I* was here?"

As Attorney General, Robert Kennedy had more than the usual contacts. If a member of his staff had a problem relating to the State Department, Kennedy could call the Secretary of State and speak to him directly. No previous Attorney General had such persuasive power. "There is tremen-

dous advantage," he once observed, "in having the same last name as the President of the United States."

In a conversation with a writer on his staff Kennedy once expressed his awe for those who could make a living out of words. He summed up with, "The only word the Kennedys know is *'terrific'*!"

Singer Dennis Day's wife gave birth to their tenth child at the same time that Ethel Kennedy was expecting her tenth baby. Bobby sent the Days the following telegram:

"In 1968 we will challenge you to the world's family football-team championship!"

"My views on birth control are somewhat distorted by the fact that I was the seventh of nine children."

Campaigning in a farm state in May, 1968, Kennedy remarked that he had done more to raise farm prices than anyone else:

"Just think," he said, "of the milk, eggs and bread my children consume."

In January, 1968, Robert Kennedy attended a large party given by the N. Y. film critics. Someone asked him why his wife Ethel had not come too and brought the children along. Replied the Senator, "There wouldn't be room for anybody else."

R.F.K. on R.F.K.

During his campaign against Senator Kenneth Keating for his Senate seat, Kennedy, throughout New York State, drew huge crowds of squealing, screaming and hysterical admirers. They tore at his clothes and attempted to yank locks of hair from his head. After one particularly frantic crowd delayed him in Buffalo, he arrived late at a banquet, looking disheveled, and had this to say: "I've been all over the state talking about Medicare and when I came into Buffalo tonight I thought I needed it myself."

New York's Republican Governor Nelson Rockefeller voiced his opposition to a state bill that would raise the minimum wage level to $1.50 an hour. Seizing the opportunity to tease the Governor a bit, Kennedy stated that he had nine children, and added, "I know *I* couldn't get by on $1.50 an hour and I doubt if Mr. Rockefeller could."

Senator Kennedy gave a California Pop Art poster maker permission to use his portrait on a poster. Looking at a display of other posters by the same artist, Kennedy suddenly pointed to one of Richard Burton and announced, "If you can make me look like him, that will be fine."

In 1962 Attorney General Robert Kennedy was presented with an honorary scroll by the Philadelphia Fellowship Commission. In accepting it he commented:

"Whenever I receive an award or am present when other people receive an award it takes me back

to my days in high school and in college—which was not so long ago. You know, when the graduating class gave the award for the best athlete and for the best scholarship and for the person who was best in Latin, and best in Greek, and who wrote the best composition—I received a prize for being the fellow with the fifth best sense of humor in my graduating class."

Philadelphia, Pennsylvania
April 3, 1692

When Robert Kennedy decided to run for the Senatorial seat from New York State, the possibility of defeat worried him. He expressed this concern to an aide by observing, "I don't want to become a retired elder statesman at thirty-eight."

Following his climb of Mt. Kennedy in 1965, Robert Kennedy came back down to earth with these remarks: "I am no mountain climber. My family has always shared an active interest in all sorts of athletic endeavor, but I personally never had thought of climbing a mountain. Frankly, I don't like heights."

Although New York Democrats anxiously awaited his decision, Senator Robert Kennedy refused to proclaim publicly any preference for a Democratic candidate to run against Republican Governor Nelson Rockefeller in 1966. Queens County District Attorney Frank O'Connor eventually was chosen, but his campaign was poorly fi-

nanced and poorly backed. During the campaign O'Connor frequently chided the Governor for his "famous name" and for his renowned fortune. On one such occasion Kennedy publicly ribbed O'Connor, saying, "Careful, Frank. We're not against *all* famous names or *all* wealthy candidates, are we?"

Early in 1966 a member of Senator Robert F. Kennedy's large office staff remarked, "We chew loyalty pills" in response to the suggestion that working hours in the Senator's office were rather long.

That remark did not go unnoticed by Kennedy, who as a Christmas present gave each of the 25 girls a small gold bracelet charm shaped like an aspirin. "One a day—RFK" read the inscription on one side of the pill, while on the other side the word "loyal" was spelled horizontally and vertically, with both words sharing a single "y" in the center.

On October 2, 1966, Senator Robert Kennedy made a guest appearance on the David Susskind Show, a television discussion program which also features questions from members of the studio audience. One such gentleman asked the Senator, "When Mr. Susskind introduced the program at the beginning, he referred to you as the number one political figure in the country today. And several recent polls are reported to have shown that you are personally more popular with the voters than President Johnson. How do you explain the fact that you are rated higher with the voters today than the President?"

Replied Kennedy, putting on his most blasé expression, "Charm, wit. . . ."

As a Senator from New York, Robert Kennedy once observed that there seemed to be a close alliance between the entertainment world and politics in that state. He speculated in 1965 that many New York politicos might be quite at home on Broadway or television.

"For instance," suggested the Senator, "John Lindsay starring in *All in Good Time;* Adam Clayton Powell as the lead in *Catch Me if You Can;* Mayor Wagner and Governor Rockefeller in *The Odd Couple* or *Two for the Seesaw;* Senator Javits in *Fade Out-Fade In;* and Winthrop Aldrich as the lead in *The Man From UNCLE.*

"Finally," concluded Bobby, "they're writing a new version of *Luv,* co-starring President Johnson and me."

Robert Kennedy knew that in order to win the 1964 Senatorial race he would have to rid himself of his image as a cold and calculating politician, an image he felt was inaccurate and undeserved. He was successful enough to win the election, after which one reporter asked him whether he was relieved to be done with the grueling campaign. "Yes," replied Bobby, who then smiled and added, *"Now* I can go back to being *ruthless* again . . ."

Johnson City, New York, is noted for its many shoe factories. During a stopover there on one of his 1964 campaign tours, Robert Kennedy claimed, "I've done two important things for the shoe industry. First of all, eight small children need a lot of shoes. And second, *I'm* the one who popularized those fifty-mile hikes."

When, in July 1964, Robert Kennedy was asked whether he would consider entering into Massachusetts politics, he shook his head negatively and replied, "I'd be a carpetbagger there."

Near the end of his 1964 Senatorial campaign in New York, Robert Kennedy sent a sample of his handwriting—barely legible at best—to a handwriting analyst. The sample said, "If you tell your readers what you see in my handwriting, you'll cost me the election."

When Bobby Kennedy stopped at Batavia, New York, for a Senatorial campaign speech, he noticed a group of six young girls who carried a sign proclaiming that they were from a nearby town called Kennedy. Said Kennedy, "You see? They talk about my being a carpetbagger, and I even have a city named after me."

Because Bobby Kennedy had been preceded to New York by a reputation of ruthlessness and cynicism, his 1964 Senatorial campaign planners informed him that they would attempt to portray him to the television audience as a sincere, generous man.

Queried Kennedy, "You going to use a double?"

Although Republican Senator Kenneth Keating was the New York *Times'* choice in the 1964 Senate race in New York, this factor did not trouble Robert Kennedy too much. "Well, at least they can

never say I got *my* job through the New York *Times.*"

Leaving the Overseas Press Club one evening, Robert Kennedy suddenly found himself surrounded by a group of nuns. "It's one of the great unsolved mysteries," remarked Kennedy. "All the nuns love me and none of the priests do."

Early one morning, before leaving home, Senator Kennedy carried the newspaper upstairs to his wife. Returning downstairs, he turned to a friend and said:

"That's my good deed for the day. Now I can go back to being ruthless."

"It gives me particular pleasure to take part in this annual observance of Law Day in Virginia. I am not only a resident of Virginia, but I came here fourteen years ago as a student—and I hold Mr. Jefferson's university at Charlottesville largely responsible for any gaps or lapses in my knowledge of the law."

> *Law Day Ceremonies of the*
> *Virginia State Bar*
> *Roanoke, Virginia*
> *May 1, 1962*

As John Kennedy's 1960 Presidential campaign manager, as Attorney General, and as an alleged "carpetbagging" New York Senator, Robert Ken-

nedy had gotten used to taking a great deal of name-calling. But at a public affair, when motion picture producer Dore Schary introduced him in particularly glowing terms, Bobby rose and dryly observed, "I've been called a lot of things in my life, but this is the first time I've been called 'beloved.' "

After speaking to a group of students from Columbia University who were visiting Washington, Senator Kennedy was asked what he thought about the current gold problem. After making a few pertinent remarks, he summed up with:

"I got a D in economics."

On the day that Robert Kennedy resigned as Attorney General a ceremony was held for him at which two Special Forces sergeants presented him with a green beret. A member of the Special Forces then attempted to give a speech but could not concentrate due to a persistent thumping originating from behind a closed door. Kennedy finally interjected with, "Don't worry about that. That's just a gorilla I keep in there." He walked over, flung open the door, and out ambled Brumus, his huge Newfoundland dog.

When speaking before a student audience during his campaign for the Presidential nomination, Senator Kennedy was asked, "What have *you* done to deserve to be President?"

Kennedy paused, then smiled. "Well, for one thing—I've cut my hair."

A professor at Harvard, recalling the days when Robert Kennedy had been his student, remembered him as having a good sense of humor. Kennedy had handed in a paper that was not very good and attached was a note, "Dear Professor: Here's that paper you've been waiting for with baited breath!"

"The state that brought moviemaking to a high art . . . has produced the new phenomenon of the actor as candidate, and a successful candidate at that. I think this is no accident. The cost of campaigning has become so high that to make a candidate and his views well enough known in a state like California or New York is impossible without either a well-known personality or enormous sums of money.

"As an unknown, virtually without funds, I was, of course, an exception."

From an address delivered at
Skidmore College
February 22, 1967

In a speech delivered at a commencement in 1963,
the youthful Attorney General noted:

"Remembering my own graduation from college—which, people keep reminding me, wasn't very long ago—I think I can imagine something of what you feel this afternoon."

Trinity College
Washington, D.C.
June 2, 1963

Senator Kennedy was much beleaguered by charges of being "ruthless." However, he often quipped about it and the day after his defeat in Oregon during the campaign for the Democratic Presidential nomination, a young girl ran up and asked him how he felt being the first Kennedy to lose an election. Kennedy later joked:

"If I were really ruthless—I would have kicked her in the instep!"

Through the years, Robert Kennedy had become somewhat sensitive about the "ruthless thing" —as he called it. So when Senator Joseph Clark was puzzled once by an over-formal letter of thanks for a small favor, Kennedy explained himself thus: "I'm just concealing the ruthless side of my nature!"

In Nebraska during his 1968 campaign for Presidential nomination, RFK spoke to a crowd on a Nebraska street. He summed up with, "On election day, if you treat me well, I'll be like the sign on your local movie theater." All heads turned to look at the marquee which read, "The Happiest Millionaire."

Senator Kennedy remarked to actor Dustin Hoffman that he hadn't yet seen Dustin's movie, "The Graduate," and then added, "But then again, you haven't seen me in the Senate."

Senator Kennedy, during the winter of 1968, gave an ice-skating party for his staff at Rockefeller Plaza. After speaking to them, he later remarked:

"I hope you noticed how I said 'New York' instead of mumbling it—as I used to do three years ago!"

President Kingman Brewster, Jr., of Yale University received a complimentary copy of Senator Kennedy's book, *To Seek a Newer World,* and inscribed on the flyleaf was the author's message, "To my good friend, Brewster Kingman."

It just so happened that Brewster was no great admirer of Kennedy and took the opportunity to rib one of Kennedy's friends about the Senator's *faux pas.* It wasn't long before the word got back to Kennedy and he immediately wrote Brewster (his name right this time) a letter of apology for the mistake and then signed,

"Sincerely yours, Kennedy Robert."

While campaigning for the Democratic Presidential nomination, Senator Kennedy of course spoke of the serious problems confronting our nation. But he also included in his speeches a sizeable amount of humor. He informed one audience of the following:

"I was sick last year, and my friends in the Senate sent me a get-well card. The vote was 42 to 41."

In 1965 Robert Kennedy held the attention of America for his celebrated conquest of Mt. Kennedy. He later recounted that near the summit, although exhausted, he felt relieved. He said, "I only had three choices—to go down, to fall off, or to go ahead. I really only had one choice."